ENDORSEMENTS

"For years, I have watched in awe as God has favored Lisa and allowed her to carry the message of His favor and goodness around the world. As you read this book, you will be captivated and inspired and your faith will soar as you learn how to walk in divine favor. Your life will never be the same! I highly recommend *Finding Favor* and her ministry."

Pastor Tim Walker
Church Alive
Middleburg Heights, OH

"If anyone knows about favor, it is Lisa Elliott. I have watched her ministry from the beginning and have never seen anyone walk in such favor. Lisa has true childlike faith and a heart for children. She has proven that with God all things are possible.

After being given one building after another, feeding the masses, suppling children with backpacks, Easter shoes, and bicycles through tears and joy, her life is testimony that she is God's little girl. Lisa lives under an open heaven and brings signs and wonders to the few and to the masses. *Finding Favor* will open your eyes to the simplicity of being a carrier of unlimited blessings and true divine favor."

Dr. J. Tony Slay
President, Ministry International Institute
LaFollette, Tn

"Lisa Elliott is a true example of one who seeks after the heart of God. I've had the honor of knowing her for over a decade and it's been such a blessing to witness the anointing and favor of God on her life. That favor is contagious. I have personally been a recipient of the overflow. I highly recommend *Finding Favor*. It will give you a glimpse into a life of favor and ignite your hope in God who makes the impossible possible!"

Dr. Lakisha Foxworth
Grace Inspired Counseling Services, LLC.
West Palm Beach, Fl

"As a board member for The Center of Hope Ministries since 2013, I have witnessed Lisa's heart to help the lost, hurting, needy, sick and suffering. During her ministry, she has helped multitudes come to know that God is real and loves them. Lisa has faced and overcome numerous challenges in her own life in order to be obedient to God. Lisa knows how to petition God for her own needs as well as for the needs of God's children. I encourage you to read *Finding Favor* and be encouraged that God loves you and that His favor is available to you!"

Bishop Dr. John Pearson
Executive Secretary, Ministry International Inc.
Clinton, TN

Ruth
To my favorite
Teacher & councler.
Love
Lisi Elliott

HOW TO WALK IN & RELEASE
THE ANOINTING OF GOD'S FAVOR

FINDING
FAVOR

LISA ELLIOTT

LIFEWISE BOOKS

FINDING FAVOR
How to Walk In & Release the Anointing of God's Favor
BY LISA ELLIOTT

Published by:

⚙ LIFEWISE BOOKS

PO BOX 1072
Pinehurst, TX 77362
LifeWiseBooks.com

Cover Design and Interior Layout | Yvonne Parks | PearCreative.ca

To contact the author | LisaElliottMinistries.com

ISBN (Print): 978-1-947279-61-2
ISBN (Ebook): 978-1-947279-62-9

DEDICATION

I dedicate this book to my three daughters:

Ashley, Sarah and Emily Grace.

God favored me when He gave me each of you.

SPECIAL THANKS

I would like to give a special thank you to the Lord Jesus Christ. It's an honor to serve You and the people You send into my life. My heart is full of thanksgiving for the love and favor You have shown me.

TABLE OF CONTENTS

FOREWORD

Finding favor with God and walking in His favor should be a priority for every born-again believer. We are totally dependent on the grace of God for every area of need in our lives. As Paul said, *"In Him we live and breathe and have our being."*[1] He already has all we will ever need and wants us to trust Him for those needs – and find favor in His sight.[2]

I am grateful to my friend, Lisa Elliott, for writing this book on how we can all find favor with our God. James said, *"Every good and every perfect gift is from above, coming down from the Father of Lights."*[3] Since every good thing is a gift from God, we need to discover how we can position ourselves to receive His gifts in every situation by finding favor with God. I believe this book can make a huge difference in your life when you apply the truths it contains.

Joan Hunter
JoanHunter.org
Author | Healing Evangelist

A NOTE FROM THE AUTHOR

I am so excited you have picked up *Finding Favor*. You are about to embark on a journey where you'll learn how to walk in God's favor and receive the anointing that goes with it. Your faith will be lifted as you read the miraculous things God does through His favor. I look forward to hearing about your own experiences and encounters with God's favor as a result of what you discover in these pages.

To share your story with me, send an email to lisa@ lisaelliottministries.com.

In Him,

Lisa Elliott

CHAPTER 1

THE ANOINTING OF FAVOR

"You have made me as strong as a wild ox: You have anointed me with the finest oil."

Psalms 92:10

The Inspiration

We were on the road headed to a revival in North Carolina when my husband looked over at me and said, "You need to write a book because God has done so many incredible things in your life."

Right before he said that, the Lord had spoken to me saying, "I want you to go into the churches and teach people to walk in My favor and release the anointing of favor." I also heard

Him say, "You can only teach what you know, and you only know what you have experienced. You have experienced My favor, so write a book on favor."

I had felt the anointing of miracles come upon me in revivals and crusades, and felt the anointing to preach God's Word. I had never felt anything like the anointing of favor.

When it comes upon me, it's like Christmas time. I know something is going to happen, but I don't know exactly what. There is such an excitement with the anointing of favor and God does something marvelous every time.

Divine Ideas

In August of 1999, we opened Center of Hope Ministries, a place where those in need could receive food, clothing and prayer. People began flooding in and I quickly realized we needed money immediately to feed them. I began to pray that God would give me ideas. While I was in prayer, He gave me several ideas. The first was an auction. That week, a man and his wife walked into the ministry and said, "This would be a great place for an auction." I soon found out this man was an auctioneer and needed a venue. He ran our auctions monthly for about seven years.

I decided to take the next idea to one of our ministry's board of advisors. He was a Christian, and a very prudent businessman who owned one of the largest car dealerships in the area. One day, I met him at his dealership. As I was opening the door to enter the lobby, it happened. The anointing of favor came all over me. I thought maybe he was going to give me one of these new cars on the show room floor. I just knew something was going to happen and I was excited.

I sat down in his office and told him I had an idea and asked if I could share it with him. He agreed. I began to share with him the idea of hosting a charity golf tournament and wanted to call it the "The Center of Hope Golf Classic". While I was speaking about the commercials, sponsors and all the details of the plan, God spoke to me. He said, "He sees more in you than you see in yourself." I knew it was God's favor.

This businessman was very intelligent and a learned listener. He never said a word. After I finished, he picked up the phone and called the local television station and set up a meeting. He wanted commercials on primetime to promote the ministry fund raiser and he would give away a free car for a hole in one! As a result of this encounter, we had the Center of Hope Golf Classic for several years. The golf course even donated exclusive use of their location for the entire day. It was amazing how much favor we had with these divinely inspired ideas. We were able to impact more families and children by obtaining the resources to expand the reach of our ministry.

> One of the purposes of favor is to
> demonstrate God's love.

With this golf idea alone, we were able to feed 100,000 people per year. We became overwhelmed with donations of clothing, furniture, and household items. Even more amazing, as we met their physical needs, we were also able to meet their spiritual needs. In the first three months we were open, we led approximately 500 people to the Lord. We began to see people delivered and set free from drug and alcohol addiction.

Miraculous, Healing Favor

In the second month of ministry, I woke up with a feeling that the Lord wanted me to fast. I obeyed with a sense of expectancy. In the past when He asked this of me, someone would be delivered or healed. As I went into the mission that day, there was a grandmother who was raising her eight grandchildren. She asked if I would pray for her 9-year-old grandson. He had a cancerous tumor behind his left eye. Doctors had only given him one year to live, and that year was up.

I asked if she could go get him so we could lay hands on him and pray. She said, "Yes," and brought him in. This beautiful brown-haired, brown-eyed boy was blind in his left eye. I asked him if he knew Jesus. He shyly replied, "Yes, my granny has taken me to church some." I asked if he had ever asked Jesus into his heart, and he replied, "No."

We first prayed the prayer of salvation with him and he received Christ. I asked him if he believed that Jesus could heal him, and he responded, "Yes." We anointed him with oil and laid hands over his left eye. I prayed that Jesus would curse the cancer at the root like He did the fig tree, and that He would restore this young man's sight. I felt the power of God, and knew he was healed. When I removed my hand, he exclaimed, "I can see!" God had healed him of cancer and opened his blind eye.

After we rejoiced and thanked God for the miracle, the little boy looked over and saw a handheld fan lying beside me. On it, was a picture of Jesus praying in the Garden of Gethsemane. He looked at me and asked if he could have the fan. He was in awe of the picture of Jesus. I told him, "That is Jesus. That's who saved you and healed your eye." This was just one of many healing miracles God performed throughout the years of our ministry.

Confirmation

About a year later, the same grandmother came into the mission (as she did weekly for her groceries and clothing), and I had the chance to ask how her grandson was doing. She had a great report. When she took him back to the clinic, the doctor confirmed the tumor was gone and her grandson could see perfectly. There was no sign of cancer!

One thing touched me the most. The grandmother told me that he sleeps with that fan on his chest every night.

> On that miraculous day I knew,
> the little boy had found favor with God.

Favor to Save a Nation

There was a Jewish woman in the Bible named Esther. She lost both her parents at a young age and was raised by her cousin Mordecai. She was courageous and feared God. Esther set such an example to all of us. She bravely obeyed God.

Here's part of her story:

> *"And the king loved Esther above all the women,*
> *and she obtained grace and favor in his sight*

more than all the virgins; so that he set the royal crown upon her head, and made her queen instead of Vashti."

Esther 2:17

Esther found favor with the king and, as a result, was able to save her people from a destructive plot to kill them all which was initiated by one of the king's advisors.

CHAPTER 2

FAVOR WITH GOD AND MAN

"You will have Favor and a good understanding in the sight of God and man."

Proverbs 3:4

God granted favor to many great men and women in the Bible, but His favor was always given to bring something forth. Below is a list of several examples you can study on your own. I encourage you to look for the purpose of God's favor in these verses.

- David brought forth a throne.[4]
- Mary brought forth the son of God.[5]

- Noah brought forth an ark.[6]
- Moses brought forth the Israelites from captivity to the Promised Land.[7]
- Esther was given Favor to save a nation.[8]
- Abraham brought forth many nations.[9]

From the Bank to the Barn

After opening The Center of Hope, I remember God speaking so clearly to me. One day in the first month of ministry, I was home cleaning the house and I thought I would take a break to read my Bible. When I opened it, it turned to the book of Esther and I heard the Lord say, "I have given you the same favor as I gave Queen Esther."

I said, "Lord, she saved a nation."

Then I heard the Lord say, "And so shall you!" In that moment, I felt the anointing come upon me.

> When the anointing comes upon you, it is for God's people and His purpose.

I was a banker for twelve years. On my way to work one day, I began to pray saying, "God, there has to be more than this. If you will use me while I'm young, I will do anything you ask." God immediately gave me a vision. I was with my family in a building with many trees growing inside. There were pallets of food, tables stacked with clothes, and bags of clothing all over the floor.

I felt as if the Lord dropped something into my spirit and I felt His presence very strongly. I realized I was in the parking lot of my work, and couldn't even recall driving there. When I got to my desk, I called my husband and told him what happened. He said, "If you can show me a building with trees in it, then I'm in!" Even I acknowledged it sounded crazy, but I knew it was God and I knew He had given me an assignment.

So right then, I decided to put in my two-week notice because I knew God was ready to use me. I didn't waste any time. That evening we went to look at buildings. I'm a visionary; so of course, I was looking for a big beautiful building. My husband, who is more of a realist, pulled the car into a gravel parking lot right off the main road. There sat a big, red barn that had been turned into a business. It had a "For Rent" sign in the window.

I thought, "He has got to be kidding me!" He pulled our minivan right up to the door and shined the headlights inside. He got out and looked through the glass. He motioned for me to get out and join him. Reluctantly, I got out of the car thinking this was a waste of time.

I looked through the front door and I couldn't believe it! As far as we could see, there were trees supporting that old barn. He looked at me and said, "I'm in." It was just as God had shown me in the vision. We both felt the power of God all over us. We got the name and number of the realtor, and made a call to him that night.

Favor with Man

Through the realtor, I found out who owned the barn. It turns out it was a man that I had gone to school with from my hometown. The very next morning I went to get my barn. On the drive up to his office, I prayed God would give me favor with this man and that he would be in his office. I also prayed that God would give me a business plan.

I walked into his office and there he was. I sat down and told him I wanted the big, red barn he had on Chapman Highway. He laughed and said he would love to give it to me, but the land was very valuable. I felt the Lord's favor come upon me and immediately I spoke.

"I will take the barn if you give me the first three months rent-free, and bring the rent from $1,800.00 a month to $1,000.00."

He looked at me and said, "I'm not sure why I should do this, but I'll take it." So now we had a big empty building for our ministry.

A few days later, I collected clothes from my home and took them to the barn. I met a couple from our neighborhood at a garage sale and told them about the vision. They came down to the barn and soon became my best and only volunteers. They shared our story with the pastor of their small church which happened to be closing their food pantry.

> They gave us three wooden bookshelves and some canned goods which became the start of our food pantry.

On the way to pick up the shelves and food, we passed a business that had desks, chairs and office furniture in the parking lot. I turned in and one of my volunteers followed behind me. I went in and asked them what they were going to do with the office items. They said they were renovating their offices and were going to dispose of all of them.

I asked if we could have them and they said, "If you can haul them away today, they are all yours." Two of us loaded large metal desks, office chairs, filing cabinets and more all day. On day three after obtaining the barn, we now had a very small pantry, a rack of clothes and lots of desks and chairs. We were excited! We were moving by faith and God was blessing us.

The lady helping us with the furniture told me about a woman preacher who had a ministry to help the poor. This lady claimed this woman of God had favor with God and favor with man. I thought of Proverbs 3, one of the chapters my mother insisted we had to memorize in our younger years.

I got my Bible out and there it was, the scripture I used to quote as a child. *"So shall you find favor and good understanding in the sight of God and man,"* [10]

I looked at her and said, "If that lady can have favor with God and man, I believe we can too." We prayed for favor and stood on His Word every day. And we began to walk in the anointing of favor. It was awesome. As I thought of something we needed, it would appear. Someone would bring it in.

The barn had no heat and no air conditioning. I would often preach in shorts and a t-shirt in the summer and my coat and gloves in the winter. The volunteers would often work bundled up on those cold days when you could see each other's breath. One cold winter day, I decided to pray that God would give us heat.

While I was there working, a truck pulled in with a camper on the back. I walked out and asked if I could help them. They asked, "What kind of place is this?"

I explained, "We are a mission and help people in need." They asked me what I needed and I said, "We need a heater. It's freezing in there." The couple looked at each and smiled. The gentleman got out and headed to the back of the truck. He opened the door and there sat a brand-new kerosene heater and a container of kerosene.

He told me they decided to take it back to the store because they changed their minds about it. He carried it in for me and we had a praise party with Jesus for about five minutes. Then the phone rang. I answered the phone. A lady said she heard we helped people in need. She then told me she had a baby and two other small children. They were living in a trailer with no heat. She asked if we could please help her.

The whole time I was listening to her voice, I was looking at that brand-new heater. I told her I would have someone deliver it to her in a few minutes. The next day, she called and thanked us. She said, "We are so warm. Thank you so much." That week another truck pulled in and dropped off seven heaters. I had never seen the driver before. But I praised God for His favor and for those heaters.

In May of 2000, we were having a tent revival just outside of the barn. I had invited Dr. Tony Slay to minister and felt the Lord tell me to also preach one of the nights. I shared from the book of Job, and my message was called, "How are you going to react to the big attack?" I felt the fire of God come upon me. The Holy Spirit was leading me to pray for people to be filled with the Holy Ghost.

The first time I ever preached, God filled 27 people with the Holy Ghost and they all soon became part of our church. The next night, Dr. Tony was preaching and I walked into the barn to get a drink of water.

I heard the Lord say, "Clear out the front of the building and have church."

I said, "Lord, who would pastor a church in a barn?"

He said, "You will." I couldn't believe God was speaking to me to pastor a church, especially in a barn. I shared this word with two close friends, but that was it.

In the beginning of my ministry, my level of faith wanted multiple confirmations. So, one right after another, the people began to come. The next day after receiving the word, a woman pulled up to the ministry with a beautiful Kimball piano. She said she wanted to donate it for "our church." I said, "We are a mission, not a church."

She answered, "God told me to donate my piano for your church." We accepted it and placed it at the front of the building where God told me to hold our meetings.

Next, a man pulled in with 52 folding chairs in the back of his truck. He said his church wanted to donate the chairs to our church. I said, "We are not a church, but we can use the chairs for the people."

The very next day, a man came in carrying a big box of old hymn books. He said, "We thought you could use these for your church." The following day, a man pulled in with a long trailer full of church pews.

We had never seen any of these people who donated these items. The Lord led each of them to give us everything we needed for our church. My assistant, Gail, and I thought this rapid sequence of donations was crazy. I looked at her and said, "If we get one more thing in here for a church, I'll set a service for this Sunday and preach my first sermon as pastor."

About that time, Gail's husband, Don, came in from doing a donation pickup from a garage sale. He said "You're not going to believe what is on my truck from this yard sale." He yelled out, "A pulpit!" I held up my end of the bargain and we held a church service that next Sunday with our family and seven other people.

We have seen miracles like this almost daily for years and still are experiencing God's favor in a phenomenal way.

CHAPTER 3

UNDESERVED ACCESS

*"After this I looked, and, behold, a door was opened
in heaven: and the first voice which I heard was as it
were of a trumpet talking with me; which said, Come
up here, and I will show thee things which must be
hereafter."*

Revelation 4:1

Favor to Enter the Throne Room

In August of 2018, I was in a revival in West Palm Beach,
Florida where I preached my first revival in 1999. I was
teaching on the Courts of Heaven. Every night, we would
go into the sanctuary to pray after everyone had left. The

pastor is like a sister to me and every time we get together, something supernatural seems to happen.

As I lay on my face before the Lord, I began to weep. We were so hungry for more of God, we were seeking His presence. As I began to raise my head, I noticed I was in His throne room. The floor of this room was unlike anything I'd ever seen. I could barely raise my head because of His glory but also, I felt afraid of being before God. I knew He was on the throne. I began to weep even more and went into repentance.

I found myself pleading for mercy for myself and my children. I noticed as I lay there trembling, I was dirty and my clothes were also. I saw my children and grandchildren in the distance. They were bound. I then felt as if someone was walking down to me from the throne. When I looked over, I saw the feet of Jesus. I knew they were His because there were nail scars in His feet.

I heard, "Those that wait on Me, become one with Me." He reached down, took my hand and helped me to stand. Immediately, all fear left me. Instead, I was overwhelmed with so much love.

When I looked at His face, I said, "I've loved You since the first time I saw You." I remember when I received Christ as my Savior at age nine. I was at the altar during a revival. The heavens opened and I had a vision of Christ. I wept for days.

I fell in love with Him then, and I am still in love with Him to this day.

I heard a beautiful sound of the most peaceful singing. Instantly, I knew it was the heavenly choir. The Lord began to dance with me. As I looked into His eyes, they were like deep pools of compassion. I felt saturated with His love. I looked up and saw two angels drop a white robe over me. I looked down at myself and I was spotlessly clean. I couldn't help but look again at His scarred feet as we were dancing. I knew that He had suffered that pain for me. And I loved Him even more.

I also noticed my feet had become beautiful like when I was a young girl. I felt so loved and so free. I looked down and saw a necklace had been put around my neck. It appeared to be a fiery, red ruby. I said, "Lord, You've given me wisdom."

He spoke from within because His mouth never moved. I heard His voice, "You asked for it."

In the far distance, I could see my three daughters and my grandchildren. They were bound. As I looked into His eyes, they were suddenly freed and began to dance and worship. Then I saw my grandson as a young man dressed all in white, preaching. I knew God's love had set us all free. This most incredible experience changed me; I knew I would never be the same. I loved Him even more than ever before.

> He favored me with access to
> free my family from bondage.

Become a Slave to the Master

A few years ago, I was in Africa for some time. The last day, I decided to stay alone, fast, and seek His presence before our late-night flight out of the country. I was on the floor praying when I felt like someone pulled my spirit-man out of my body and took me to the throne room. I was being carried by two rather large angels. I heard a loud voice saying repeatedly, "Become a slave to the Master. Become a slave to the Master." Then I heard, "You are an oracle of God!"

When my spirit came back into my body, there were two angels over me. Both were kneeling on the floor. On one side, one was touching my heart while the other was touching my mouth. I laid there in awe of what I had experienced. I felt the glory of God all over me.

Favor Brings Access

There is a realm in the spirit where I believe God desires us to enter. He spoke to me once as I was traveling into Africa saying, "You have open access to the throne room and open access to the store house." Years before, He had showed me my storehouse in heaven. It looked like a warehouse, and inside was everything I needed for this life here on earth. There were all the spiritual gifts of 1 Corinthians 12. Everything I needed for my family, home, buildings, vehicles, provision, were available.

> God doesn't want us struggling to believe for things that are already ours.

Favor to Dream

At the age of nine, I began to have prophetic dreams. One of these dreams returned several times from the age of nine until thirty-two. Sometimes I would have it numerous nights in a row, then I may not have it for a few weeks. But the dream was always the same.

> *I walked into this large room and shut the door behind me. I then walked up a very large curved stairway. I remember noticing the steps had no support under them. Each time at this point in the dream, I wanted to turn around and go back, but in my heart, I knew I had to keep going until I reached the top. As I approached the top of the stairway, I saw a window. I knew*

this window was my only way out. The window opened and I stepped out barefoot onto this beautiful grass in a peaceful meadow. Beside the meadow was a flowing river. The dream always brought me peace.

At age 32, I went through a very difficult time in my life. One day that year, I was praying in the spirit while cleaning our home. As I entered the kitchen, I had a vision. I saw the exact window from my dream, but this time the Lord was there.

He reached and took my hand and walked with me. I said, "Lord, You were never in my dream before."

He replied, "I was always there!" Now, anytime I want to go there, He is there for me.

The Bible says, *"And He will be called, Wonderful Counselor, Mighty God, Everlasting Father, Prince of peace."* [11]

When you find God, you find peace.

CHAPTER 4

FAVOR BY ASSOCIATION

"A man's gifts make room for him
and brings him before great men."
Proverbs 18:16 NIV

While I was living in Ghana, West Africa, God granted me such favor with great leaders. One was the Archbishop Duncan Williams. Bishop Williams told me that he didn't just let anyone visit his home. Somehow, I found favor with him. I was humbled just to be sitting in the same room with such a great man. He is one of the most honored and anointed men in all of Ghana, known through many countries as well as the United States. I had first heard him preach at one of

Bishop T.D. Jakes' Woman Thou Art Loosed conferences years ago.

Favor with Kings, Presidents and Key Leaders

Bishop Williams told me I was to come to Ghana and train under his ministry because God was sending me to the nations. So, I went and trained under his leadership. Bishop Williams is known for being a general for strategic prayer for all nations and I can attest the man can pray. He carries a very heavy anointing and walks in a realm of authority that scares the devil.

As I trained and served under him for over ten years, God gave me favor to both be around him and to sit on many platforms with him. The Ghanians love God and respect the anointing. I was given favor with the people simply because of my association with the Archbishop. This association provided large platforms and open doors to preach places I wouldn't have otherwise been given. I often found myself at the dinner table with presidents, kings and other great people of influence.

During one event called "The Impact Conference," I was blessed to be in the living room of Bishop Williams' home with several of my favorite speakers and musicians. Bishop T.D. Jakes, Pastor Paula White, Noel Jones, musician Donnie

McClurkin and many other anointed people. I knew I was there not because I was anyone great but because I had favor with God and favor with man.

None of them knew me or probably even noticed me. I had nothing I could claim that would move any of these mighty generals of the faith. Despite my obscurity, I was always introduced as Papa's daughter which made me feel special. But even more that, I couldn't help but feel humbled.

> Those of us in that room had two
> things in common: God's favor
> and a personal mandate.

Favor is for Establishing Kingdom Relationships

God has given many men and woman favor with someone of influence to propel them where they need to go to accomplish their assignment. We all need relationships with people to be blessed and to be a blessing. God showed us His abundant favor when He sent His Son to accomplish His will in the earth which included His relationship with us. This is the most important relationship we can have, cherish and develop.

You may meet someone today that is tied to your destiny at some point but maybe not for today or tomorrow. God will bring these key relationships back around for the appointed time. Often, God works in ways we never expect. We have to trust Him and treasure those relationships, not for what we can get, but for what we can give. It's always in the giving of ourselves and our substance that we are blessed.

> *"In everything I did, I showed you that by this kind of hard work we must help the weak, remembering the words the Lord Jesus himself said, 'It is more blessed to give than to receive.'"*
> *Acts 20:35 NIV*

CHAPTER 5

FAVOR COMES
TO THOSE HE CHOOSES

"For many are called, but few are chosen."
Matthew 22:14

As part of the Body of Christ, we are all called to serve. God has given us the necessary gifts and talents we will need to fulfill our destiny. It is our act of service to Him to use them for His glory.

In 1 Samuel 16, Samuel went to the house of Jesse in search of God's chosen king for Israel. Jesse had eight sons but he only presented seven of them to Samuel. Jesse couldn't see his young shepherd son, David, as a logical choice for king.

"Jesse presented seven of his sons to Samuel. But Samuel said to Jesse, 'The Lord has not chosen any of these.' Then Samuel said to Jesse, 'Is that all of the young men?' Jesse replied, 'There is still the youngest one, but he is taking care of the flock.' Samuel said to Jesse, 'Send and get him, for we cannot turn attention to other things unless he comes here.' So Jesse had him brought in. Now he was ruddy, with attractive eyes and a handsome appearance. The Lord said, 'Go and anoint him.' This is the one!"

1 Samuel 16:10,12 NET

"When they arrived, Samuel noticed Eliab and said to himself, 'Surely, here before the Lord stands His chosen King!'. But the Lord said to Samuel, 'don't be impressed by his appearance or his height, for I have rejected him. God does not view things the way men do. People look at the outward appearance, but the Lord looks at the heart.'"

1 Samuel 16:6-7 NET

When you are chosen by God,
it doesn't matter what you look like, or
where you're at.

When it is your time for His anointing to pour over you, willingly open your arms and heart to receive it and obey the voice of the Lord.

When you carry God's favor, you can receive unmerited selection over others even when you don't meet the qualifications. You stand on platforms you don't deserve to be on. You may even receive money from people who don't like you. I've had that happen to me.

One man came into the barn and said, "I don't believe in women preachers at all, but I'm going to write you a check." Many times I have heard things like, "I don't know why I'm giving this or doing that, but I just know I have to." The favor of God opens doors and hearts, and causes people to respond for your good.

Favor is Attached to Your Assignment

Just like we saw in 1 Samuel, there was a king in David even when he was still tending sheep. He may not have known it was there, but God put everything in David which was needed for his assignment as king. He also gave David favor to fulfill his destiny.

Despite this heavy opposition, the anointing of favor allowed David to take down the giant, properly deal with King Saul and to defeat the armies that came against him. Ultimately, he was given favor to rule his nation. The favor of God caused him to be loved by many.

Why was David chosen over all his brothers to receive the favor of God and be anointed to become king? Because his heart was after God. That was all the qualification needed to be blessed with God's favor.

How Do We Walk in the Favor of God?

All the leaders I've studied in the Bible who accomplished great things have five things in common.

1. Love for God – *"Love the Lord your God with all your heart and with all your soul and with all your mind and with all your strength."* [12]

2. Obedience – *"Now if you obey me fully and keep my covenant, then out of all nations you will be my treasured possession. Although the whole earth is mine."* [13]

3. Submission – *"Submit yourselves therefore to God. Resist the devil and he will flee from you."* [14]

4. Prayer – *"Therefore I tell you, whatever you ask for in prayer, believe that you have received it, and it will be yours."* [15]

5. Chosen – *"But you are a chosen people, a royal priesthood, a holy nation, God's special possession, that you may declare*

the praises of Him who called you out of darkness into his wonderful light."[16]

The anointing of favor causes ordinary people to do extraordinary things.

I have always had a heart for the things of God. He has shown me much favor. I didn't earn it, and I've definitely not deserved it. But I see it has been given to many ordinary people like myself so He could be glorified in the extraordinary things that He does through each of us.

"Before I formed you in the womb I knew you: before you were born I sanctified you, and I ordained you a prophet to the nations."
Jeremiah 1:5 NKJV

Our ministry mission would never have been able to reach so many people for Christ or help the needy if we tried to do it in our own ability. As I reflect back, I can't help but see how blessed we were to serve so many, and how God's grace and favor was and still is on our ministry.

CHAPTER 6

FAVOR CAN BRING OPPOSITION

"Now Israel loved Joseph more than any of his other sons, because he had been born to him of his old age: and he made an ornate robe for him. When his brothers saw that their father loved him more than them, they hated him and could not speak a kind word to him.
Genesis 37:3 NIV

Joseph's dream didn't get him into trouble, but telling the dream did. You have to be careful who you share your dreams with. The more favor you walk in, the more haters you will have.

Joseph's brothers plotted to get rid of him. They stripped him of his coat, but not his favor. They threw him into a pit and sold him as a slave for twenty shekels of silver to the Ishmaelites who dragged him off to Egypt.

The brothers then slaughtered a goat and dipped Joseph's robe in the blood. They took the soiled robe back to their father and told him an animal had torn Joseph to pieces. They thought that was the end of him. Joseph's father wept and found no comfort. He even said, *"I will continue to mourn until I join my son in the grave."*[17]

It is astounding to me that when you're anointed with favor, those that are closest to you seem to hurt you the most. When a stranger comes against you, it's painful. But when the attack is from family, it's an issue of the heart. The devil will use whoever he can get to destroy your dream, even those of your own house.

> *"Wrath is cruel, anger is overwhelming,*
> *but who can stand before jealousy?"*
> *Proverbs 27:4 NIV*

Joseph went from a home where he was loved and cared for to being thrown into a pit and sold into slavery by his own brothers. These were the same ones he grew up and played with as a child. The ones he dined with, slept beside and worked with every day. It would seem he was the only good thing that came out of that family.

Maybe you have been rejected, abandoned or sold out by a person close to you. Someone you trusted or loved betrayed you. Joseph had to learn quickly to forgive those who hurt him or bitterness could have easily taken over his life.

Favor brought Joseph out of slavery to the palace where he served as an advisor and right-hand man to the king. During Joseph's years of growth and promotion, Joseph's family was experiencing famine. Jacob sent his sons to seek favor and food from the Egyptian king. Without recognizing Joseph, the brothers bowed down to him begging for food just like God had showed him in his dream so many years before.

Because of the forgiveness in Joseph's heart and knowing what God's favor on his life had done for him, he was able to save his family and be reunited with his father. No matter what the opposition or the battles you face in life, God has favored you for a reason. The end result is His blessings and fruit.

> When you have favor, sometimes you
> may experience the down side
> of jealousy and opposition.

When the Lord anointed me with favor, people came against the ministry. Some became jealous and angry because God gave us certain buildings they wanted.

I remember one example when God told me He had yet another building for us. We had just been blessed with a $350,000 building that very day. I was so excited about what God had just given us that I couldn't imagine getting another one. Out of obedience to God's voice, I called a realtor friend and told him I was looking for a building in that area, maybe a church. He said, "I just listed a church three miles from your house."

I said, "You show me a church three miles from my house and I'll buy it!" He gave me the address and there it was, a beautiful, white church with a bell tower only three miles from our home.

Don't forget, we had outgrown the barn where we had been ministering for 2.5 years, sometimes four times a day with no heat and no air. When I walked into this church, I could see it packed full with me standing in the front preaching the good news of the gospel. I asked the realtor the price, then looked at him and said, "My Daddy is rich and He gets me anything I need." We truly needed this church to give the people a place to worship in comfort.

After we left, I tried to figure out how we could come up with the purchase price. I loaded up my three daughters and headed back to the church that evening. I walked around the property and prayed that if it was God's will, He would give it to us. My girls were not far behind me. I immediately stopped because I felt as if God was standing toe to toe with me. I heard Him speak, "This is a ministry of favor." I knew we were getting this church. God saw my heart, heard my prayers and answered. He was providing this beautiful building as our church's new home.

A few days later, I met with the realtor, gave him a $1000.00 check for earnest money and made him a ridiculously low offer for the church. Later, he called to say the church owner had accepted my offer. We had no money and we were in the process of moving into a warehouse that had been donated to the ministry. But I kept going, remembering that God said, "This is a ministry of favor."

We started our loan process by faith. The banker called me to announce we were approved for the loan. That was a miracle within itself. But then he said, "The appraisal shows the value of the property is much higher than what you are paying for the building. Unless you want to put something down on the building, you don't have to." I couldn't believe it! God's favor gave us a beautiful church building. In fact, when we closed on the property, the banker gave us a check back. This was the favor of God.

Overcoming Opposition

I didn't know until later that other organizations wanted the same building and were attempting to purchase it. So, even though God blessed us, the building did come with some opposition.

With two locations of ministry, we were reaching more people for Christ. The warehouse was filling up and so was the church. People were being fed, clothed and saved.

> But with this growth and expansion came great opposition.

While pastoring in our new building, I was hospitalized three times in the first month alone. The third time, I was in the emergency room waiting to be admitted to the hospital. Suddenly, I saw a large angel standing over me. I began to cry. However, the angel brought me such peace that I knew I was going to be okay.

For three days, I lay helplessly in that hospital bed. I couldn't feed myself or go to the bathroom without assistance. I felt so weak. On the third night, I woke up to the sound of clanging metal. I couldn't lift myself up, but I opened my eyes to see the back of a warring angel. It had a sword in its hand which he was swinging up and down. I could see the light from above my bed reflecting against the steel of the sword.

I knew there was a battle going on for my life. Immediately, I felt strength come to my body and I sat straight up in bed. I shouted, *"I shall not die but live, and declare the works of the Lord!"*[18]

The next day, the doctor walked into my room and appeared to be quite shocked. I was totally healed. He discharged me from the hospital. The Lord favored me and sent an angel to war for my life. I praise Him for His favor and His grace.

One day during our Back to School distribution, we were about to hand out 1,000 backpacks full of school supplies and new shoes to kids in need. I was in severe pain with kidney stones and I broke out in a cold sweat. I truly thought I was going to die. I went to the bathroom and passed two visible kidney stones. With the pain dissipating, I got myself together and returned to the church activities. By His grace, I was able to lead 54 children to Christ that day.

Miracles on the Mission Field

God sent us to the international mission field to minister and meet the needs of His people. My mother did mission work over the years, so I had heard many miraculous stories but not one about any opposition. I had heard many times that the devils are always bigger in other countries. Since doing mission work, I am inclined to agree.

I've faced such great opposition on the mission field from spiritual warfare including bot flies, severe dehydration, to malaria. But on the upside, God favored me and put me in position to reach thousands of people. We saw blind eyes open, deaf ears healed, and people come up out of wheelchairs.

In one year, we saw 8,000 people saved in Ghana, West Africa.

The Doctor

I remember a trip to Guadalajara, Mexico with a ministry team. We always prayed for God to protect us, to use us for His glory and give us favor with the people. I was scheduled to preach every night for twelve nights. We did see God do many miracles. Once, over thirty people came up with back pain including a lady with a hunch back. I heard the Holy Spirit tell me not to touch anyone. As I passed each one, I began to hear bones crackle and pop, and the woman with the hunch back stood straight up and began to dance. It was a powerful night.

The third day, I awoke to 27 mosquito bites on my right arm. The bites were very painful and began to worsen that day. The pastor and his wife told me there was a visiting doctor coming to their church that day to see people who needed medical assistance. As we sat in the church waiting on the doctor to see me, my arm continued to swell and I felt even worse.

I looked at the door of the church as a very thin frail man in a dress jacket entered the building. I immediately heard the voice of God say, "Tell the doctor I'm going to heal him today."

I thought "I'm the one sick, Lord. He is the doctor." Despite my feelings, I looked at the interpreter and told him what the Lord said so he could communicate it to the doctor. The doctor looked down and I noticed a tear rolling down his right cheek.

He looked at my arm, gave me some medicated cream and sent me back to the pastor's house where I was staying. He said that he would return later after he finished with his other patients. On the way back to the house, I asked the Lord, "What is wrong with the doctor?" The Lord showed me what looked like an x-ray. The doctor's esophagus was closed and he could not swallow food or liquids.

Soon the doctor came to the house and as he walked in, I felt God's favor. I knew God was going to give this doctor a miracle. Through the interpreter, I shared what God showed me. The doctor said, "Yes, it is true." He was a former star athlete who had had a stroke three years prior to our coming. It had closed off his esophagus and made him bedbound for the first year. He wasn't able to eat or drink even a teaspoon of water.

As he pulled back his jacket, he showed us a feeding tube in his abdomen. He said he felt as if he was starving all the time. We anointed him with oil and prayed for him. The *prayer of faith will save the sick, and the Lord shall raise him up: and if he has committed sins, they shall be forgiven him.*[19]

> God opened the doctor's esophagus.
> He was healed by God's grace.

Earlier in the day, I had made a soup for the team to eat, so we warmed him a bowl and brought him a glass of cool water to drink. I said to him, "God has healed you. Eat." He looked at me and slowly lifted the spoon of soup to his mouth. He swallowed, paused and then begin to weep with tears of joy!

When you experience opposition, you have to fight against it. Miracles lie in wait for us on the other side of our obedience and perseverance. Because I pressed back against the opposition I was experiencing, God gave this dear doctor a new esophagus. Now he could eat, drink and be merry. We all sat at the table, wept and praised God as the doctor ate the whole bowl of soup and drank the entire glass of water. What a day of rejoicing we enjoyed!

God's love has also set me free from a broken heart. In fact, His love has healed me of 39 sicknesses. He has brought me through surgeries, out of car wrecks, up off my death bed in the bush of Africa and continues to keeps me safe. I always feel like God's love for me is overwhelming. At times, He makes me cry. When you're associated with God, there is glorious supernatural favor. And if someone's heart truly belongs to God, they have His love as well. God gives us this love that goes far beyond what we can comprehend.

> *"And to know this love that surpasses knowledge, that you may be filled to the measure of all the fullness of God."*
> *Ephesians 3:19 NIV*

CHAPTER 7

FAITH AND FAVOR

"Now faith is the substance of things hoped for,
the evidence of things not seen."
Hebrews 11:1

You can have faith in God and not have favor. But you can't have favor without faith. Favor causes the most ordinary person to live in an extraordinary way. Faith will also. They go hand in hand. Favor will cause you to believe. I love the following scripture and live by it every day.

> *"We've not seen God, but we believe in Him. 'But*
> *without faith it is impossible to please him: for he*
> *that cometh to God must believe that He is, and*
> *he is a rewarder of them that diligently seek him.'"*
> *Hebrews 11:6*

When you fall in love with someone, your heart wants to please them. When you marry, and your love grows throughout the years, you want to please them even more. When you know you have disappointed the one you love, you hurt all over. That's how our relationship should be with God. If faith is what pleases Him, then I want to stretch my faith to the fullest to please Him even more.

From Four Counties to Four Nations

The Lord favored us with four locations of ministry. One location is the large distribution ministry in East Tennessee. By 2003, we were in four counties helping families in need as well as opening up food pantries in impoverished areas throughout the U.S. In 2006, the Lord spoke to me saying, "I'm taking you from four counties to four nations!" That word seemed so big and so impossible. Because of His blessings in the past, I waited with great anticipation. When God speaks about your future, He will give you the grace for the place you are going. Trust Him and be obedient to His will for your life.

Trust and obedience bring more favor.

The doors to the nations began to open. One day while I was on my riding lawn mower, God spoke to me, "I'm sending you to Ghana, West Africa on September 13th for one year and I'll use you mightily." God ordered our steps and opened the doors. I was at the training center the day before we left for Africa and I admit I was battling with this decision. We were leaving the comfort of our home, our ministry that we loved and, more than that, our children and two small grandchildren.

I was crying out, "Lord, have we not given food, clothes, and furniture away to the poor? Have we not given bicycles away to children? Have we not opened food pantries all over the U.S.?"

He answered, "Yes, but none of that has pleased Me."

I stopped crying and asked, "What, Lord? None of this giving has pleased You? Then what pleases You?"

He answered, "Your faith, now that pleases Me." I was shocked! In my mind, everything we had already done required faith. It took faith to step out to leave my job as a bank manager. It took faith to register recipients for our Christmas and Back to School giveaways before the supplies were even there.

Stepping from one location to another without anything but His Word pleased Him. Knowing this, we chose to trust Him and journeyed to Africa for a year. He revealed a people and a place that needed what we had.

When God Shows You a Need, It's Your Opportunity to Meet It

Over the years, we have been able to bless many children through the ministry. One hot summer day, my husband and I were taking our girls to get a cold drink at a gas station. We pulled in and I couldn't help but notice a small, skinny boy as he rode up on an old rusty bike. The seat was taped together and the bicycle wobbled as he rode in. He was only wearing a pair of shorts. No shirt or shoes. He walked up to the counter and paid for one piece of gum.

My heart was so moved by what I saw. I wanted to give him the five dollars I had in my hand, but didn't know how to do it without making him feel uncomfortable. I went back to the car almost in tears. I looked at my husband and said, "Did you see the little boy with the old bike? Someday I'm going to buy brand new bikes for children in the rural areas."

My husband looked at me, smiled and said, "You're going to save the world, too. Aren't you?"

I replied, "A small part of it."

God Pays for What He Orders

We opened the doors of our ministry in August of 1999. After I saw the little boy who needed a bike, I began to raise money for bikes. By that Christmas, we were able to purchase 263 new bikes for children in our rural area. The following year, we did a radio-thon and raised $43,000.00 in 22 hours. The ministry was able to give out over 1000 bicycles.

For the next eleven years, we did this same fund raiser in the Appalachian mountain area and gave over 11,000 bikes away to children that had never had a bicycle before. We registered the children by faith and God would move on their behalf. God gave us phenomenal favor with the local radio station and the listeners. We were blessed to raise $100,000.00 a year which allowed us to give toys, bicycles and food away to over 4000 children. This was favor for the children to be blessed.

> The most incredible thing about our Christmas giveaways wasn't the thousands of bikes; it was the hundreds that came to Christ through them.

Favor Brings Another Building

My friend Kristie and I were on a plane headed to West Palm Beach, Florida. I was to preach a revival and she was going to lead the worship. I was given the window seat, my friend sat to the left of me, and a lady sat in the aisle seat next to her. Kristie began a conversation with her and I heard Kristie ask, "Are you from Florida?"

The lady said, "No, I actually live in Tennessee now, but I work in Fort Lauderdale." She said she made a trip to Tennessee and fell in love with it, so she went to her boss and asked if she could move.

He told her, "You can live anywhere you want as long as you do your work."

I was still looking out the window but I couldn't help but hear that part of the conversation. I felt like the Lord was saying that to me. So, quietly in my heart I said, "Lord, if I could live anywhere in the world as long as I do your work, I want to live in West Palm Beach!"

When I got to the church, the pastor said she hadn't been feeling well for a while. She asked me to come because she wasn't able to speak. The Lord directed her to reach out to me. I had done revivals there for about fourteen years and loved her and the church family very much.

I began the revival and the prophetic was stirring in me strongly. As I was speaking prophetically and praying over the congregation, I saw a caravan of angels coming to take her out of there. I shared what I saw with her. She looked at me and asked, "Does that mean I'm going to die?"

I couldn't believe she said that, but then I felt what it meant. God showed me abnormal cells like under a microscope. I heard the word "hemoglobin". I thought the vision meant she was moving, but not dying. She was only 57 years old.

I told her I wanted to take her to a good doctor and she agreed. As we drove an hour to Fort Lauderdale for her appointment, I encouraged her and prayed the whole way. I noticed she wasn't praying or fighting. Pastor Phyllis had always been a woman of prayer. It reminded me of a time when I was going through a battle in my body. When I told God I was tired of fighting, He said, "If you don't fight, you don't win."

When we got to the clinic, they did an MRI and some more tests. The doctor came back to tell us that she had stage 4 cervical cancer. She acted as if she already knew.

I drove her home, took her inside and stayed to pray for her some more. She was a dear friend to me for years. I was heartbroken. I asked her why she wasn't fighting. She told me that she was tired of fighting and she seemed to have peace. I told her I would continue the revival if she wanted and she agreed it was the best for the people.

It was Sunday morning, the last day of the revival. I was standing to the side of the platform and I heard the Lord speak to me, "You will pastor here." It took me back. I looked at Kristie with the look I get when God speaks to me. She knew God said something to me. It was difficult to step up to preach that morning knowing their pastor was dying and the people didn't have a clue.

I was trying to see myself there. I had never lived anywhere but Tennessee. It was my home. What about my three daughters? I was flooded with questions. I told Kristie after church and again, it was if she knew. I looked at her and said, "If God wants me to pastor here, I want twenty confirmations," and laughed. Well, God began to give me confirmations before I walked out the door.

> To walk in His favor, we must be obedient to what He assigns us to.

Monday, I went to Pastor's house and she was very weak. She looked at me and said, "Pastor Lisa, God spoke to me to give you the church. I know I can trust you with the people." I promised her I would do the best I could to teach and shepherd the people. On February 3, 2011, my dear friend, Pastor Phyllis Brandon, at the young age of 57, was taken into heaven only ten days after she was diagnosed with cancer. She was a blessing to so many. It was an honor to be given the church, but even more, that God saw enough in me to allow me to pastor the best congregation in West Palm Beach, Florida.

Faith to Walk on Water

Two years after accepting the church, I walked into a Christian bookstore one day and saw a picture hanging on the wall. It was Jesus walking on the water. I stood there staring at it and said, "Lord, I want to have faith to walk on water." A tear rolled down my cheek thinking of how that level of faith would please Him. I asked the clerk to take the picture down so I could purchase it. It still reminds me of how much faith God requires of us.

> *"Shortly before dawn Jesus went out to them, walking on the lake. When the disciples saw him walking on the lake, they were terrified. 'It's a ghost,' they said and cried out with fear. But Jesus immediately said to them, 'Take courage! It is I. Don't be afraid.' 'Lord if it's you', Peter replied. 'Tell me to come to you on the water.' 'Come', He said. Then Peter got down out of the boat,*

walked on the water and came toward Jesus.
But when he saw the wind, he was afraid and,
beginning to sink, cried out, 'Lord, save me!'
Immediately Jesus reached out his hand and
caught him. 'You of little faith.' He said, 'Why
did you doubt?'"

Matthew 14:25-31 NIV

The disciples' faith was tested to see what was hidden in their heart. This test exposed the fear and doubt that were there. Yet how could the disciples doubt after they had already seen Jesus perform so many miracles? Fear is the opposite of faith. The Bible tells us to "fear not" 365 times, one for every day of the year.

Cancer, Walk Through It

Only two weeks after I had stood in that bookstore asking God to give me faith to walk on water, I was diagnosed with ovarian cancer. As I was leaving the doctor's office, I asked the Lord, "What do I do?"

He replied, "Walk through it." I remembered how Peter stepped out on the water. As long as his eyes were on Jesus, he could stay up. But when he looked at the storm, he began to sink. If you think about it, Peter didn't really walk on the water, he walked on His Word.

> If we heed the voice of God and step
> out by faith on what He says to us,
> we won't go under.

We can walk through anything. I had His Word. Not only that, I had a vision of me going to the nations. I knew I wasn't going to die until I finished my assignments from God, my Father. The diagnosis was three malignant tumors with one attached to my left ovary. The MRI also showed a 22 cm mass in my stomach and lymph nodes which were abnormal in size. I was having terrible pain in my lower back. Many times through the four-month process, I felt that I wasn't going to make it. However, I had learned over the years not to trust feelings, but to trust God. I hung on tightly to His promises, His Word.

Favor to Live

God delivered me from death and took away the cancer. The surgery showed no mass in the stomach even though it was on the MRI. They ended up doing seven surgeries over a two-year period. But I am cancer-free, and God gets all the glory.

CHAPTER 8

MARY'S MANDATE

"And the angel came in unto her and said, 'Hail
thought are highly favored, the Lord is with thee:
blessed art thou among women.'"
Luke 1:28

Some of the most ultimate favor is found in the story of
Mary, the mother of Jesus. Out of all the women on earth,
she was given the mandate to give birth to the Son of God.

> *"In the sixth month of Elizabeth's pregnancy,*
> *God sent the angel Gabriel to Nazareth, a town*
> *in Galilee, to a virgin pledged to be married to a*
> *man named Joseph, a descendant of David. The*
> *virgin's name was Mary. The angel went to her*

and said, 'Greetings, you are highly favored! The
Lord is with you.' Mary was greatly troubled at
his words and wondered what king of greeting
this might be. But the angel said to her, 'Do not be
afraid, Mary: you have found favor with God.'"
Luke 1:26-30

Wow, could you imagine an angel appearing to you to deliver a message from the throne room that you were going to become pregnant by the Holy Ghost? Mary was a virgin, yet became pregnant with the Son of God! Through this visitation and birth, all humanity changed. What a holy mandate for this young lady from Galilee.

Have you ever thought, "Why her? What was it about Mary that she would be chosen for such an incredible assignment?" By studying her life in the Word, we learn who she was and the characteristics that positioned her for this honor.

1. **She was a servant.** *"'I am a servant,' Mary answered. 'May your word to me be fulfilled.' Then the angel left her."*[20] We must be willing to serve God and serve people. Mary went to Elizabeth and served her for about three months even after she had the visitation of the angel. The greatest people are those who have a servant's heart.

2. **She was humble.** *"For He has been mindful of the humble state of His servant. From now all generations will call me blessed."*[21]

3. **She was obedient.** *"Behold, to obey is better than sacrifice."*[22] She obeyed the voice of the angel and submitted to the will of God for her life.

> God knew Mary and created her for this purpose.

God knows what is in you and how strong you are. He knew you before your birth. I believe He gives each of us a mandate as He creates us. Just think how Mary went from being a humble servant known by a few, to being a woman recorded throughout history in His Holy Bible. She had to be humbled and at the same time excited that God chose her to carry, give birth to, and raise the Messiah.

You can't be willing to serve but not willing to suffer for your mandate. I can't imagine what Mary must have felt as people noticed her belly growing and began talking about her around town. When you carry greatness, people will talk. They will look for you to fail. When you are pregnant with destiny, the closer you are to it coming forth, sometimes the harder the challenge.

Just as a woman who carries and bears a child, there is pain mixed with victory. When Mary's labor pains came, there was no hospital, hotel, motel or bed and breakfast where she could rest or deliver her baby. There was no doctor, midwife or medicine to ease the pain. I wonder if she ever thought, "I didn't ask for this," but knew it was necessary for her call. Finally, Mary and Joseph arrived at a stable full of animals, hay and straw, a humble quiet place where she would give birth to the Son of God.

The Bible tells us in Matthew Chapter 2, wise men came and brought valuable and foretelling gifts of gold, frankincense and myrrh for Jesus. Can you imagine what went through Mary's mind as these extravagant gifts were laid at their feet?

CHAPTER 9

FAVOR CAN GET YOU WHAT MONEY CAN'T BUY

"Give, and it shall be given unto you; good measure, pressed down, and shaken together, and running over, shall men give into your bosom. For with the same measure that you meet with all it shall be measured to you again."
Luke 6:38

Pickle Jar, Pickle Lane

Luke 6:38 was the first scripture God gave me when I started ministry in August 1999. I was in my kitchen cooking dinner for my family. My mind was full of questions concerning the details of ministry. I asked God, "Who will fund this ministry?"

He said, "I will, through the people." He said, "Get the pickle jar out from the bottom of the cupboard and put Luke 6:38 on it and everything you need will come through this jar." I got the pickle jar out, found the scripture, typed it out and taped it on the jar.

The next day, I was on my way to the mission, pickle jar in hand. I walked in and placed the large pickle jar on my desk which was up front near the entrance. Everybody who knew me laughed at my jar, but everything we needed came through that jar. Half of the time, we felt the money appeared supernaturally.

> Favor draws people in and causes them to do things they don't always understand.

One day, I saw a taxi pull up and a lady got out. She looked as if she needed help. We were closed at that time of day, but I opened the front door to ask if I could help her. She looked at me and said, "No, but I can help you!" and handed me a roll of money. She then got back into the taxi, left and I never saw her again. It was just enough to pay the rent for the barn that month and it was due the next day.

It's All About Obedience

After about two years of taking up donations in the pickle jar, I got a call and a man asked, "What do you need?"

I just blurted out, "We need a building."

He said, "I have one. Could you come over to look at it?" He didn't tell me the address, just what business it was beside.

I was so excited I felt the anointing all over me. I loaded up my volunteers and said, "Let's go look at this building."

We had been in a season of offering up a prayer of thanksgiving every day thanking God for our "big building with loading docks". We had been believing for one because we had out grown the barn and really needed loading docks to unload the trucks. We pulled up to this big white warehouse with loading docks and two semi-trucks.

We met the man in the parking lot and he told us the story about his father passing away. They had listed the building on the market to sell for $350,000 or lease for $3500.00 a month. He explained he had not received one inquiry about the building. On his way to work that morning, he made a list of non-profits he could possibly donate it to.

In his car that morning, he began to pray. About that time, a red minivan passed him with a sign on the side that read,

"Center of Hope - Feeding America's Hungry Children." Driving the other direction, he saw a green van with the same sign which was one of our volunteers. He jotted down our ministry name and phone number at the top of this list. Then he called me.

We walked into this big, open warehouse with no heat, no air, and not even a window. He told me that if we wanted to use the building, it was ours as long as we wanted, for FREE. He would pay the taxes, electric and water. And if we needed food hauled, he would help us with that, too. We started crying and thanking God. He then handed me his business card.

As I looked at it, I asked, "Is this the address to this building?"

He answered, "Yes, 2612 Pickle Lane."

I heard the voice of God say, "It's all about obedience."

God had tested me to see if I would be obedient to use an insignificant pickle jar to receive offerings. He gave us favor with a truck driver to give us the use of a building on Pickle Lane. So, if God asks you to do something that seems strange, do it. He will bless your obedience!

> Favor brought forth a building with loading docks and semi-trucks that we didn't pay for but needed to feed His people.

Blessing for Obedience

> *"If you fully obey the Lord your God and carefully follow all His commands I will give you today, The Lord God will set you high above all nations on earth. All these blessings will come upon you and accompany you if you obey the Lord your God."*
> *Deuteronomy 28:1-2 NIV*

> *"You will be blessed when you go in and blessed when you go out. (v6) The Lord will grant you abundant prosperity. (v11) The Lord will open the heavens, the storehouse of His bounty, to send rain on your land in season and to bless all the work of your hands. You will lend to many nations but will not borrow from none." (v12)*

If people would obey the Word and voice of God, they would walk in the blessings of Deuteronomy 28:1-14. I know, because I have experienced these blessings throughout my life. I have learned when God has something for me to do, whether it is difficult or not, He will give me the grace to accomplish it and bless my obedience. Trust and obey Him, and the blessings will come.

Sow a Seed for Something New

One day I heard the Lord say, "Break the connection." I immediately saw the face of the building owner flash before my eyes. I didn't understand, but I knew we were to leave the building. The owner's family were wonderful Christian people and were obedient to bless us with the use of their building for two years, but it was time for us to move.

I had no idea where we would go. Our board of directors respected that I heard from God, but still they were concerned. This was a free building but we had outgrown it and God knew what was coming. When I entered the mission that day, the Lord spoke, "Sow a seed for something new. Give everything in the building to another ministry and I will give you something new."

Honestly, I was devastated. As I looked around that seven-hundred square foot building, I thought, "It's so full, and our volunteers have worked so hard to organize it and make everything so nice for our clients." Then I thought, "If we give everything, what will we have to give to the people in need?"

The building looked like a mini-department store. We had a large food pantry, freezers, clothing racks, a large shoe department and furniture. Everything was free for the people. The Lord was saying, "Get rid of it. Give it away." My mind went back to the scripture the Lord first gave me, *"Give and it shall be given…"*[23] At that point, I was willing to do anything He asked because I trusted in Him fully and knew nothing was ours. It's all His anyway. He simply entrusted us to be its keeper for a time.

I called the lady who had the ministry we were giving to. When I shared how the Lord told me to give her everything in the building, she screamed in my ear. She began to shout and praise God. I walked outside, got in my car and checked the messages on my phone. There was a message from a store in town saying, "This is Mary with Indian Gap, could you come to the store?"

I drove out there and told the lady who I was and that I had received a message to come in. I had never been in the store before because at that time, I couldn't afford their things. It was an upscale store, and everything in there was beautiful. Mary came, shook my hand and said, "I guess you know we are going out of business. We want to donate everything in the store to your organization." In my mind, I thought:

> "I sowed a seed of a warehouse full of used stuff, and in return God blessed us with a store full of NEW stuff. This could only be God's Favor."

God is so good. Before we could pick up the new racks and clothes, the barn was empty. God was telling us to leave. Where do we go and where do we take this semi-truck load of new stuff? Our church building couldn't hold it.

Favor for Millions

I went to the airport with my assistant, Tonya, to take care of some business. On our way, as we were passing a certain building on the main road, I felt the Holy Spirit lead me to stop. I called the number on the real estate sign and in a short time the agent showed up. I asked him the price of the building and he said it was two-and-a-half-million dollars. He asked me who I was but I didn't give him my card or my name. I looked at him and said the same thing I said to the realtor for the church building we purchased in 2001, "My Daddy is rich, and He gets me what I need, and we need this building."

"But my God shall supply all your need according to His riches in glory by Christ Jesus."
Philippians 4:19

I could see dollar signs in his eyes as he smiled from ear to ear. As I walked through the building, I felt I had been there before. I then remembered a vision the Lord showed me many times while working in the barn.

In the vision, I was walking down a long hallway which connected thirty rooms. In those rooms were small groups of people. Then I stepped into a large room full of young adults who were standing in worship. Then I stepped into another wing of the building and there was a large congregation of people from many ethnic backgrounds, rich, poor, young and old. I was standing on a raised pulpit preaching the gospel. Over the sanctuary was a prayer room where people were lying face-down in prayer, interceding for every service.

I realized I was walking in the very building God showed me eight years before. It was 26,000 square feet with 17.9 acres located near the airport. It was just what we needed for where we were going.

I asked the realtor, "How many offices are there?"

"Thirty." he answered.

Then I asked, "Does it have an upstairs?"

He answered, "Only one over the training room." That would be the prayer room I saw in the vision. This building had been a business, not a church, but God had another plan. The realtor asked, "So you've been here before?"

I said, "No" even though I had spiritually been there several times in the vision.

Without any doubt, I knew this was where we would be because God had shown it to me. I asked him, "Who owns the building?" Being a real estate agent before, I knew that was information that was not supposed to be shared, however, he handed me the owner's card.

I felt favor come upon me so heavily. I told him I would get back with him, and asked if we could just walk around the grounds. He said, "Yes," and left.

I looked at Tonya and said, "Let's lay hands on the front of the building and pray." We did just that. We prayed God's Word.

> *"Again, truly I tell you that if two of you on earth agree about anything they ask for, it will be done for them by my Father in heaven."*
> *Matthew 18:19 NIV*

Tonya and I agreed it would be done and God would give us favor with the owner. I called him while standing there on the front step of the building, I told him I was at his building and had met with the agent, but I would like to meet with him. He said, "I'll be right there." I felt the favor of God and knew He was moving on our behalf. A car pulled up. Out stepped a short Chinese man. I shook his hand and introduced myself and my assistant.

> Favor will cause people to do things and not know why they're doing it.

I had seen God move so many times, I knew He would do it again. I told the owner what our non-profit was about and that we needed the use of his building for our Christmas distribution for about five months. He said, "It's sitting here empty," and handed me the key. He added, "But if it sells, you understand you would have to leave." We agreed.

Within an hour of pulling into that building, God gave us favor with the owner and the key to use this building for free! The owner didn't ask for proof to see if we were legit or anything. It was phenomenal favor. God blessed our obedience and faith and proved once again that He could provide anything we could believe Him for.

CHAPTER 10

FINANCIAL FAVOR

*"But you shall remember the Lord your God: for
it is he that gives you power to get wealth, that he
may establish his covenant which he swore to your
fathers, as it is in this day."*
Deuteronomy 8:18

It is the Lord who gives us the power to get wealth. He gives
us ideas, creativity and gifts to work with. We can be one idea
or one relationship away from being empowered for wealth.
Wealth is an abundance of valuable possessions or money.
The state of being rich. There are over 2000 references in
the Bible concerning money. So, it's important to have it

available. The more you do for God, the more favor and faith you need to fund it.

> *"A feast is prepared for laughter, and wine makes life happy, and money is the answer for everything."*
> Ecclesiastes 10:19

If we trust in the Lord, He will supply everything we need.

Favor Can Bring Forth Finances

When we first started the ministry, I didn't even think about the money it would cost to fund what God had called us to do. But it didn't take long to see that everything costs something. We have always prayed that we would be the most-favored ministry in all the world. Not because we wanted to get somewhere or be somebody, but the vision God has given us is big and it takes financial favor.

A man named Mac used to come into the ministry and donate food over the years. Every week, he would come to the loading dock and unload canned goods. He was kind of grouchy, and had one shirt he wore almost all of the time with a small hole in the shoulder. I thought maybe he needed a little help. One day he came in with his two cases of tuna and handed me a check for $1000.00. He looked at me and said, "Go buy those kids some shoes for that 'Back to School' thing you all do," and left.

Over the years, Mac became like family. I was always trying to lead him to the Lord, but to no avail. One day, I heard he was sick and I went to visit him. I was surprised to pull up to a beautiful home with a pool. "I must have had the wrong address," I thought. I went to the door and rang the doorbell. He invited me in. I set the food down that I had brought him and made conversation.

I asked him if I could help him with cleanup to which he agreed, so I jumped in and started washing his dishes. His wife had passed away about the time he started visiting the mission. They had no children so he lived alone. I made sure he was fed and explained that one of us would drop by on occasion to check on him. We loved him, and he loved what we did for the children.

A few weeks had gone by and we hadn't heard from him. We found out he was moved to a nursing home and wasn't doing well. I went to pay him a visit. He was lying there and didn't look well. I asked, "Mac, do you know we love you?"

He said, "Yes, I do." He was always a hard man to get to. He continued, "I don't think I'm going to make it much longer," and asked me to perform his funeral.

I assured him, "It would be an honor."

He began to tell me that he always liked what I did for the kids and that he was leaving me something. I started crying and told him, "I don't want anything from you. We just want you." I told him he needed to come to Christ and that's all I wanted. I stayed there by his bedside for half of the day and we continued to talk. I had known him and tried to lead him to the Lord for over eight years. That evening, he finally accepted! I was so happy. Mac came to Christ and was on his way to heaven. That was the last time I saw him.

A few days later, I got a call from his bank. The bank representative said, "Mac left something in his will for you." A few of our volunteers attended the funeral and I officiated the ceremony. The service started and the funeral attendant brought me his and his wife's flags. They had both been in the military and wanted me to have them. I quickly noticed there were only three people attending outside of us. A total of seven all together. It brought me to tears. I was so sad that no one was there for such a precious man.

The attendant then took me into a room with the bank representative for the reading of the will. The representative proceeded to read, "He has left a two-million-dollar estate." He then handed me a list of non-profits Mac had left $50,000.00 each to. The bank rep said the money was all in government bonds. He continued, "[Mac] favored your ministry over all the other non-profits, so the highest yielding bonds go to you." Ours totaled $61,000.00!

This was a precious man who spent every day buying food and delivering it to every non-profit in town. We found favor with this grumpy, old man, and grew to love him. The biggest blessing was we led him to Christ. It was a win-win situation. To God be the glory. You never know who God will use to bless you.

And Another

One day I was sitting in my office when Tonya came to my door with that sparkle in her big blue eyes and said, "Somebody is here and he is wearing a suit. He looks important and he has an envelope in his hand."

I said, "By all means, bring him back." She walked in with this businessman who had an envelope.

He said loudly, "On behalf of the Ralph Hawkins estate, you are rewarded $30,000.00." I didn't even know who Ralph Hawkins was but I knew this was God's favor.

I asked the businessman how Ralph knew of us. He said that Ralph had come in the barn when we first started and said he liked what he saw. We were so touched. We walked him out and began a Holy Ghost dance party. We were crying and praising God. God used someone we didn't even know to bless us.

> It's amazing the favor God gives to bring forth finances for the assignment, and it always seems to come right when you need it.

The Prayer of Multiplication

Every year, we held four major events at the mission. One was Thanksgiving where we fed a thousand people a hot Thanksgiving meal two days before, and then gave all the families turkey baskets to take home for Thanksgiving Day. We invited fabulous gospel groups to sing while everyone was seated at tables decorated by different churches and businesses.

Every year, we registered our clients for the dinner and baskets in faith that we would have what we needed. We were three days away from our event when I was sitting at my desk working. Tonya came down that big long hallway caring two turkeys, one in each hand. She said, "We need to pray the multiplication prayer over these two turkeys because this is all we have and we only have three days." So, we did. We prayed God would multiply those two turkeys like He did the fish and loaves of bread. We needed about 500 turkeys.

Tonya took the turkeys back to the freezer and we continued to work. Not even an hour later, Tonya came down the hall with a tall man in a suit. The man looked around, shook my hand and told me he was the senior pastor of a church in that area. He looked at me and said, "How did you get this building?"

I said, "It was just God's favor, Sir."

He said, "Are you leasing? Did you purchase it?"

I said, "No, it was given for us to use at no charge." I told him Tonya and I prayed the prayer of agreement and laid hands on the front door. Thirty minutes later, we were given the key.

He looked at me and said, "We have tried to purchase this building for four years." He shook my hand and left. About twenty minutes later, he called me and said, "Is there anything you need?"

I replied, "Yes, there is. We need 500 turkeys to feed the hungry for Thanksgiving."

He asked, "How much would they cost?"

I had the figures from the store right in front of me on my desk. I said "$3,387.29."

He said, "I'll have my secretary drop a check by."

I said, "Thank you, Jesus."

> The favor of God will bring increase. He can cause people to ask what you need and then give it to you.

God Loves to Bless Us

I was sitting at my desk at home one day preparing a sermon. I thought I would like to have a big van with a bed to travel in with the girls. I was evangelizing throughout the eastern part of the United States and it was hard for the girls and me. The thought left my mind until I got a call from my friend Dee Pinkard. He said, "Hey Lady, do you need a van by any chance?"

I said, "Dee, I was just thinking how I would like to have one.

He said, "Well, God spoke to me that Lisa Elliott needed a van." He went on to say, "Come pick it up. It's sitting in the driveway."

As I was leaving Dee Pinkard's house, the Lord spoke to me, "You can have whatever you can believe Me for"! So, we drove that van home and then, onward down the road to preach the gospel.

It was high enough to fully stand up. It had runway lights and a push button to open up the bed. It was just what we needed. God is so good. Favor with man has resulted in twelve cars being given to us to give away to families in need. Favor is the special affection of God toward you that releases an influence on you, so that others are inclined to like you, or to work with you. And it's all for His purpose.

> Favor will cause people to bless you over and over again.

Favor is For You, Too

You can walk in His favor. Start by believing His promise, *"Thou shall find favor and good understanding in the sight of God and man"*[24] as I did, and you will find it coming to you. The anointing of favor will follow you and your faith will be lifted as you see God lead and direct you into your purpose and destiny.

Favor is contagious. I have gone into churches and released the anointing upon pastors and congregations. I have seen several get new buildings and their congregations even grow in size. As you walk in favor, release it to others so everyone around you can walk in it, too.

God wants to bless you and anoint you with His favor so that you can experience Him in all His glory. He loves you. Remember, those that wait on Him become one with Him. So, wait on the Lord in your prayer time, hear His voice, and allow Him to transform you into His likeness. He has great plans for you, and the end of your life will be far greater than the beginning!

May His blessings of divine favor be upon you all the days of your life as you live with a thankful heart.

ABOUT THE AUTHOR

Lisa Elliott is an author, pastor and prophetic voice with a mandate to bring revival to the nations. She founded The Center of Hope International in 1999, opened food pantries and planted churches throughout the United States, and has been a voice against hunger since 2010 through Feed the Children.

Lisa has a heart to raise leaders and missionaries for Christ. She worked to bring better education to the Appalachian Mountains through GED and LIT programs. Lisa also started the Educate Africa Project in Ghana, West Africa in 2009 bringing many children out of the villages into schools.

Between working in miracles and speaking prophetically, Lisa carries hope and healing throughout the world through crusades, revivals and conferences. Lisa resides in the Smoky Mountains of Tennessee with her three beautiful daughters and five grandchildren.

www.LisaElliottMinistries.com

ENDNOTES

[1] Acts 17:28

[2] Hebrews 11:1

[3] James 1:17

[4] Luke 1:31-33, 69-70

[5] Luke 1:25-30

[6] Genesis 6:1-9, 9:17

[7] Exodus 6:26

[8] Esther 7:3-4

[9] Genesis 18:5

[10] Proverbs 3:4

11 Isaiah 9:6 NIV

12 Mark 12:30 NIV

13 Exodus 19:5 NIV

14 James 4:79 NIV

15 Mark 11:14 NIV

16 1 Peter 2:9 NIV

17 Genesis 37:35 NIV

18 Psalms 118:17 NIV

19 James 5:15

20 Luke 1:38 NIV

21 Luke 1:48

22 I Samuel 15:22

23 Luke 6:38

24 Proverbs 3:4

All scriptures come from the King James Version unless otherwise noted.

WORKS CITED

New Marked Reference Bible. King James Version. John C. Winston Co. Zondervan Bible Publishers, 1928,1956.

New Spirit Filled Life Bible. New King James Version. Thomas Nelson Bibles, Thomas Nelson, Inc. 2002.

The Holy Bible, New English Translation. Biblical Studies Press, 1996-2006. *BibleGateway.com,* www.biblegateway.com/versions/New-English-Translation-NET-Bible/#booklist

The Holy Bible, New International Version. Biblica, 2011. *BibleGateway.com,* www.biblegateway.com/versions/New-International-Version-NIV-Bible/#booklist.

Made in the USA
San Bernardino, CA
19 October 2018